夔門天下雄
夔門天下雄をり
Kuimen is magnificient under heaven.

3

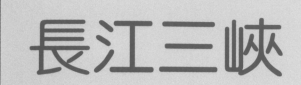

# 長江三峡

　　萬里長江從各拉丹冬走來,納千河,匯百川,浩浩蕩蕩,
東奔入海。她是中華民族的搖籃。千萬斯年,她不但以甘甜
的乳汁養育了華夏兒女,而且給我們留下無比豐厚的遺產。
她以恢弘的氣魄,堅韌的力量在崇山峻嶺中雕刻出美輪美奐
的長江三峡。于是,地球上出現一條令萬千游子留連忘返的
藝術長廊。

　　而今,勤勞智慧的華夏兒女又在西陵峡口構建起世界上
首屈一指的攔河大壩,給長江三峡增添了更加壯麗的風光。
在這里,造物與人功井放光華,歷史與現實交相輝映,人們不
但在大自然的鬼斧神工中傾倒,更在包容萬代風華的歷史醇
釀中陶醉!

　　万里の長江は各拉丹冬山から発源し,たくさんの河川
を納めて,長江に合流し,滔滔と東海に注いでいる。長江
は中華民族文化の発祥地と呼ばれている。数千年以来,昔
から長江はその水で中華民族を育てただけではなく,もの
すごく豊かな遺産が残されている。長江は雄大な気魄と
弛まぬ力で,険しい山山の中に美しい長江三峡を造り上げ
た。それで,地球上何千万の観光客が引きも切らず訪れる
芸術長廊ができた。

　　現在,勤労、智慧に富む中華民族は西陵峡の入口で世
界一の三峡ダムを作り,長江三峡に以前よりもっと壮麗な
景色を付り加えると見ている。ここに造物(自然)と人工、
暦史と現実が相互並存して,共に光りを放つと見られてい
る。人人は大自然の不思議な造物に心を動かされただけ
ではなく,さらに,長い歴史の風貌変遷に気持ちよく酔っ
てしまう。

Coming from Geladandong, the vast and mighty Changjiang River flows into the sea with its thousans of absorbed streams and rivulets. She is the cradle of the Chinese people. For thousands of years, she not only fed the Chinese people with her milk but also left them a rich and boundless legacy. She carved the Three Gorges of the Changjiang River (the Yangtze River) out of the lofty ridges and towering mountains with her broad mind and tough and tensile strength. Thus, an art gallery fascinating to tourists appears in the world.

Now, the diligent and clever children of the Chinese people start to construct the largest dam in the world across the Changjiang River and contribute a beautiful scenery to the Three Gorges of the Changjiang River. Here, the nature beauty and human creativity shine together and history and reality are merged. People not only could appreciate the craftsmanship of nature but are also fascinated by the mallowness of the Chinese historical records.

　　庫區內重慶至奉節一綫長 423 公里,兩岸自然景觀與人文景觀珠串玉連,令人目不暇接。

　　三峡ダム地区の重慶から奉節までの長さ423キロの区間に両岸の自然景観と人文景観が数珠のように連がって,人には目が及ばないほど忙しい。

　　The route from Chongqing to Fengjie in the Reservoir region is 432 km long. The landscape and human creativity on both banks of the river are too many for the eye to take in.

**重慶**　重慶位于庫區之尾,是我國西南地區的經濟中心,也是山水園林和重要紀念地的集中地。

　　重慶　は三峡ダム地区の末端に位置し,中国西南地区の経済中心で,また,山水庭園と重要な記念地が集中する所で有名。

　　Chongqing located at the end of the Reservoir region. It is the economic center in Southwest China and a concentrated area of scenic spots and historic sites.

嘉陵江索道
嘉陵江のロープウィエ。
The cableway over the Jialing River.

重慶港
重慶港
The port of Chongqing.

繁星璀璨的山城之夜
美しさに酔う山城の夜景
The starry night of the mountain city.

鬼都之門
鬼の都の門
The Gate of the Ghost Capital.

**豊都鬼城** 位于豊都縣城東北平都山上。神話中傳説,豊都為"鬼國",平都山為"鬼都",人們死后都要到此報到。主要景觀有奈何橋、天子殿、十八層地獄等。

　豊都鬼城　鬼城は豊都県の東北側の平都山に位置し,神話によると,豊都は"鬼の国"で,平都山は"鬼の都"だ。人がなくなると必ず,ここに至る。主な景観は奈何橋,天子殿,十八層の地獄などである。

Fengdu－－the City of Ghost. located on the Pingdu Mountain in the northeast of the county of Fengdu. Legend has it that Fengdu was a "Ghost Country" and the Pingdu Mountain was the "Ghost Capital". People had to report here after death. Its main scenic spots are: "Bridge of Helplessness", "Emperor's Hall", "The Eighteen-layered Hell", etc..

奈何橋
奈何橋
The Bridge of Helplessness.

鬼城索道
鬼城のリフト
The cableway in the Ghost Capital.

**忠縣石寶寨** 位于城東 45 公里長江北岸玉印山上,為 12 層塔形樓閣,高 56 米,每層三方四角,逐層內收,依山取勢,設計精巧,宛若仙山瓊閣,被譽為世界八大建築奇迹之一。

忠県石宝寨 忠県石宝寨は忠県の東 45 キロ離れた長江北岸の玉印山に位置する。12 階建ての塔形の楼閣で,高さは56メートル。各階は三方四角で,下から上まで徐徐に小さく収め,山により建てられた。設計はとても精巧で,まるで仙人が住んでいる楼閣のようだ。世界八つの建築奇跡の一つと言われている。

Shibaozhai at Zhongxian County located on the Jade Chop Mountain on the north bank of the Changjiang River, 45 km from the city. It is a tower-shaped 12-story building with a height of 56 meters. Propping against a precipice, its construction is ingenious, with a dimension of three sides and four corners and shrinks in shape story by story. It looks like a jewelled palace on the mountain of immortals and is praised as one of the eight wonderful constructions in the world.

石寶寨
石宝寨
Shibaozhai.

石寶寨接送游客的"花花轎"
石宝寨の観光客を送迎する"花かご"
The "flowery sedan chair" which meets and sends off the tourists.

**萬縣市** 西山公園鐘樓
万県市西山公園の鐘楼
The clock tower at the West
Hill park in Wanxian City.

**雲陽張飛廟** 位于長江南岸飛鳳山麓,與縣城隔江相望。始建于東漢末年,是為紀念三國時蜀漢名將張飛所建。廟內建築別具特色,館藏碑帖、文物十分豐富。

　雲陽張飛廟　張飛廟は長江南岸の飛鳳山麓に位置し,川を隔てて,雲陽町を見通す。張飛廟は三国時代蜀漢名将張飛を杞るために東漢末期から建て始められた。廟にある建築が特色を持ち,碑の対聯、文物が豊富に保存されている。

　The Temple of Zhangfei at Yunyang County　located at the foot of the Fei-feng Mountain on the south bank of the Changjiang River opposite to the county seat across the river. It was first built at the end of the East Han Dynasty in memory of the famous general Zhangfei of the Shu Han Kingdom. Constructions in the temple are unique. Collections of stone tablets, calligraphy books and relics there are very abundant.

張飛廟遠眺
張飛廟遠望
Distant view of the Temple of Zhangfei.

張飛廟杜鵑亭
張飛廟杜鵑亭
The Azalea Pavillion in the Temple of
Zhangfei.

**奉節古城** 西漢末年公孫述、三國劉備等曾在此盤桓,唐代大詩人杜甫等亦在此居留,歷史遺迹甚多,名揚海内外。

奉節古城 西漢末年公孫述,三国時代劉備などがここで滞在したことがある。また唐代の大詩人杜甫がここで居住したことがある。歴史の遺跡がものすごく多く,国内外によく知られている。

The ancient city of Fengjie. Gongsun Shu at the end of the West Han Dynasty and Liu Bei in the period of the Three Kingdoms had lingered about here and Poet Du Fu of the Tang Dynasty stayed here for a short time. They left many well-known historic sites here.

依斗門 杜甫詩雲:"夔府孤城落日斜,每依北斗望京華",據傳此門為紀念杜甫所設。

依斗門 杜甫の詩句から"夔府孤城日が落ち斜め,北斗に依る毎に京華を望む"。杜甫を記念するために建てられたそうだ。

The Yi-dou Gate. There is a couple stanza in Du Fu's poem which goes like this: "In the sunshine-slanting evening, I long for our capital by way of the Dipper". It is said that the gate was built in memory of him.

古城牆一隅
古城壁の一角
A corner of the ancient city.

11

甘夫人墓
甘夫人の墓
The tomb of Madam Gan.

永安宮遺址　今為奉節師範學校校址。公元222年，劉備伐呉兵敗，憂憤病篤，次年在此向諸葛亮等交托大業，史稱"劉備托孤"。
永安宮遺跡　現在奉節県師範学校。西暦222年，劉備が呉を討伐して敗れて，危篤におちいて，次年ここで諸葛亮などに家事、国事を託した。歴史上"劉備託孤"と言われる。
The ruins of the Yong An Palace. It is now the site of the Fengjie Normal School. In A. D. 222, Liu Bei, Emperor of Shu Kingdom, had been defeated in his invasion of the Wu Kingdom. He died here of worry and indignation the next year. On his death bed, he entrusted his son, the heir-apparent, to his Prime Minister Zhuge Liang. This is called "Liu Bei's entrusting his son to Zhuge Liang".

奉節"水八陣"　位于城東南江畔，為一長1500余米、寬600余米的狹長磧壩，傳說諸葛亮在此設陣御敵。因臨近水面，故稱"水八陣"。

　奉節の"水八陣"　奉節城の東南の河の畔に位置して，長さは1500メートル；幅は600メートルあまりのほそ長い，乱石の磯である。伝説によると，諸葛亮はここで陣取りをして，敵と対戦することで，また水面に臨むので「水八陣」，と言われている。

　The Eightfold Maze in Water. located at the riverside southeast of the city. It is a narrow sandbar about 1,500 meters long and about 600 meters wide. The legend has it that Zhuge Liang set it to resist the enemy. It is thus named because it is near the water.

白帝城遠眺
白帝城遠望
Distant view of Baidicheng.

**奉節白帝城** 位于城東4公里,瞿塘峽口長江北岸之白帝山上。西漢末年,公孫述據蜀,在此自稱"白帝",故名。

　奉節白帝城　白帝城は古城の東4キロ離れた所、瞿塘峽の入口、長江北岸の白帝山に位置する。西漢末年,公孫述は蜀を拠め,"白帝"と自称した所で,「白帝城」と名付けたのだ。

　Baidicheng at Fengjie. located 4km east of the city at the Baidi Mountain on the north bank at the mouth of the Qutang Gorge. At the end of the West Han Dynasty, Gongsun Shu occupied Sichuan and declared himself the "White King" here. Hence the name Baidi (white king).

竹葉碑　白帝城名碑之一，斯碑熔詩書畫于一爐。畫中藏詩為：“不謝東篁意，丹青獨自名。莫嫌孤葉淡，終久不凋零”。

竹葉碑　白帝城の有名な石碑の一つだ。この石碑は詩と画が一体となり，画の中に詩を含め，“東篁の意に謝らず，丹青が独自名を立つ，孤葉が淡さ嫌らず，長くしても散らずと保つ。”

The Bamboo Leaves Tablet. One of the famous stone tablets at Baidicheng. It merges poem, handwriting and drawing together. The poem is hidden in the drawing.

白帝城山門
白帝城の山門
The entrance gate of Baidicheng.

鳳凰碑　白帝城名碑之一，意蘊畫中，畫内有鳥中之王鳳凰，花中之王牡丹，樹中之王梧桐，故又名“三王碑”。

鳳凰碑　白帝城の有名な石碑の一つで。深い意味が画の中に隠している。画の中に鳥の王様と言われる鳳凰，花の王様と言われるぼたん，木の王様と言われるアオギリがあるので，「三王碑」とも言われている。

The Phoenix Tablet. One of the famous stone tablets at Baidicheng. It embodies the phoenix (king of birds), the peony (king of flowers) and the Chinese parasol tree(king of trees) in a picture. It is also named "the Tablet of three kings".

白帝城西閣
白帝城西閣
The West Pavillion in Baidicheng.

"劉備托孤"群塑
"劉備託孤"の塑像
The group of statues depicting the scene of "Liu Bei's entrusting his son to Zhuge Liang".

# 三峽風光

三峽景色　　*The Scenery in the Three Gorges*

　　長江三峽西起重慶市奉節縣白帝城,東至湖北省宜昌市南津關,全長193公里,是馳名中外的旅游勝地。瞿塘峽以萬仞之峰,顯其雄奇偉岸;巫峽以葱鬱之巒,顯其幽靜秀美;西陵峽則以洶波猛浪,顯其水惡灘險。它們次弟相接,景觀各异。峽區內重巒叠嶂,江水紆曲,古木森森,氣勢磅礴,舟行其中,有"峰與天關接,舟從地窖行"之感。游人壁立船頭,雖自渺小于立地接天的峰巒,但在偉哉、雄哉的美的感悟中自會升騰起超越時空、擁抱山河的壯懷!

　　長江三峽の西は重慶市奉節県白帝城から,東は湖北省宜昌市の南津関まで約193キロであり,世界で有名な観光地としてよく知られている。瞿塘峡は刀の刃のような峰を持ってその雄大さを誇っている。巫峡は緑に満ちた山巒で,その幽邃と美しさを見られている。西陵峡は流れが連く難所が多いことで,また,その険しさなどを表している。三つの峡は次第に連がり,見どころも違う。三峡の中,高い峰が連連と続き,長江の水が紆曲し,古木が森森と生い茂り,気勢が上がり,舟がその中を走ると,「峰は天と接して,舟が地下の洞窟で走る」という感じがある。観光客が舟頭に立つと,自分が天と接する山峰よりごく小さいがその雄大さ,美しさの自然環境中に徐徐に時間、空間を超し,美しい山河を抱くような感じが出ると思われる。

　　The Three Gorges of the Changjiang River begin from Baidicheng of Fengjie County of Chongqing City in the west and end at Nanjing-guan of Yichang City of Hubei province in the east, with a length of 193km. It is a famous scenic spot known the world over. The Qutang Gorge is magnificient with its high peaks; the Wuxia Gorge is secluded with its verdant beautiful trees and the Xiling Gorge is dangerous with its roaring torrents and shallows. They follow one after another and present different landscapes. In the gorges, there are sweeping mountains, winding currents and old trees. The boat seems to be sailing in a cellar with sky-kissing peaks overhead. Standing in the boat, though feeling insignificant beside the high peaks, you would come to realize that a lofty ideal to grasp the beautiful land is rising inside you and soaring over time and space.

**瞿塘峽** 西起重慶市奉節縣白帝城,東至巫山縣大溪鎮,全長8公里,兩岸陡壁摩天,懸削狹峙,雷鳴的江濤,給巍峨的群峰更添幾分雄渾的氣勢。古人有詩贊雲:縱有萬管玲瓏筆,難寫瞿塘兩岸山。

瞿塘峡 西は重慶市奉節県の白帝城から,東は巫山県の大渓鎮まで,全長8キロ。両岸の断崖絶壁が高く合い対峙し,雷鳴のような浪音,巍峨な峰峰にさらに雄大な気勢感を添えている。"縦に万本の玲瓏筆があっても,瞿塘両岸山の写しが難なりと,いう古詩がうたっている。

The Qutang Gorge. It begins from Baidicheng of Fengjie in Chongqing and ends at Daxi town of Wushan with a length of 8 km. There are sky-scraping precipices on both banks of the river and roaring torrents which present an imposing view. An ancient saying goes like this: Even if you have various flowery pens, you are unable to describe them well.

瞿塘之春
瞿塘の春
Spring in Qutang.

瞿塘之夏
瞿塘の夏
Summer in Qutang.

瞿塘之秋
瞿塘の秋
Autumn in Qutang.

瞿塘之冬
瞿塘の冬
Winter in Qutang.

孟良梯　峽口江南絶壁上有呈"之"字狀小孔，見方 30 厘米，自下而上直達山腰。傳說稱，北宋名將楊繼業死后葬于山頂望鄉臺，部將孟良趁夜晚鑿孔攀援而上，欲盜尸骨，后被和尚發現后伴裝雞鳴，孟良誤以為天曉，恐驚動守兵半途而廢。

孟良梯　峽口の江の南岸の絶壁の上に「之」字形の小さい穴が連なり，幅は30cmぐらい，下から山の腰まで続いている。伝説によると，北宋の名将楊継業が亡くなった後，山頂の望郷台に埋められ，部下の孟良は夜中に穴を掘って登り，尸骨を盗もうと思った時，お坊さんが発見して，にわとりのなきごえを真似した。孟良が日があけたと思って，衛兵に発見される恐れを考えながら，途中でやめた。

The ladder of General Meng Liang. At the mouth of the gorge, on the south bank of the river, there is a precipice with a line of "之" shaped square holes ($30 \times 30$cm) extending from the bottom to halfway up the mountain. Legend had it that the famous genarel Yang Jiye of the North Sung Dynasty was buried here at the top of the mountain after his death. Meng Liang, his subordinate, bored holes on the precipice and climbed up in order to steal General Yang's bones. A monk discovered him and pretended the cock's crowing. Meng Liang thought it was dawn. He withdrew for fear of arousing the guards.

倒吊和尚　位于孟良梯附近百米峭壁上，一石狀若光頭脚、肚臍外露的和尚倒挂于懸崖之上。相傳這是孟良受騙后，憤怒地對和尚進行懲罰。

さかつるしたお坊さん　孟良梯の近く100メートルぐらいの絶壁に一つの怪石がある。その形は坊主頭、裸足、へそも剥ま出しているお坊さんに似ている。崖にさかつるされている。伝説によると，孟良が騙された後，怒って坊さんに懲罰を行ったそうだ。

Hanging the monk upside down. It is at about hundred meters from the precipice of the Ladder of Meng Liang. It is shaped like a monk hanging upside down. It is said that it was a punishment to the monk angrily done by Meng Liang.

鳳凰飲泉　峽中一景，有石若鳳凰吸水。
鳳凰が泉を飲む峡谷景色の一つ。石は水を汲む鳳凰のような形で命名された。
The Phoenix is drinking. It is a scene in the gorge on a precipice, representing the phoenix drinking water from a spring.

瞿塘摩岩石刻
瞿塘摩岩石刻
Inscription carved on stones at Kuimen.

夔門天下雄,艦機輕輕過
夔門は天下の雄なり,軽舟は連く通行
Kuimen is magnificient under heaven, Ships pass withcare.

巍哉夔峽
雄大な夔峽
How magnificient Kuimen is!

瞿塘
瞿塘
Qutang.

瞿塘古棧道　位于江北懸崖峭壁,是古時陸路出峽的唯一通道。
瞿塘の古桟道　長江の北岸の絶壁に位置し,昔陸路から峽谷を出る唯一の道だそうだ。
The ancient roadway at Kuimen.

夔門古炮臺
夔門古砲台
Ancient Fortress at Kuimen.

夔門鎖江鐵柱　　史載：自唐代以來,守關大將多在夔門西口北岸崖邊立鐵柱,拴鐵鏈鎖關御敵。遺留至今的夔門鎖江鐵柱高 2.03 米,雖銹迹斑斑,似乎仍可聽見鐵馬兵戈的吶喊和敵茜被阻的哀嘆。

夔門長江を鎖す鉄柱　　史書により,唐代からここを守る将軍たちがたいてい夔門西口北岸の山崖で鉄柱を立ち,鉄のロ－7°で連なり敵を防御した。今現在まで残っていた夔門の河を鎖す鉄柱は2.03メートルの高さで,錆いっぱいが付いているが,それを通して,昔の戦場の敵陣に攻めこむときの喊声や敵方が阻まれて嘆く声が聞こえるような感じが思い浮かぶ。

Iron locking-pillar of the river. According to historic records: Since the Tang Dynasty, most of the generals who stationed here set iron pillars with heavy chains at the north bank to the west of Kuimen to barricade the enemy. The remained iron pillar today is 2.03 meters high. Although rustic, yet it reminds one to think of the battle cries of the old days.

風箱峡　江北赤甲山懸崖峭壁上，幾個洞穴内有巴人懸棺，一端置于洞口，状若風箱，故名。
風箱峡　長江の北岸の赤甲山の絶壁にある。洞窟内に巴人のお棺が入って，片頭は洞の入りロに置いて，風箱の形に似ているので，"風箱峡"と名付けたわけ。
The bellows Gorge.  On the precipice of the Chijia Mountain at the north bank of the river,  there are hanging coffins in some caves looking like bellows.  Hence the name.

陽春三月
陽春三月
The beautiful spring.

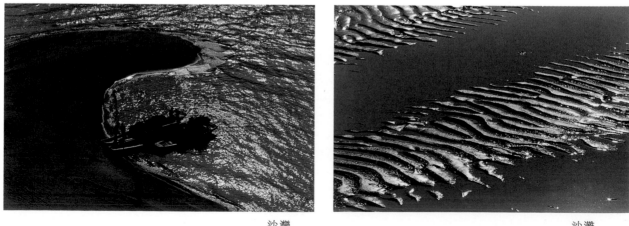

沙灣　　　　　　　　　　　　　　　　　　　　　沙灘
砂湾　　　　　　　　　　　　　　　　　　　　　砂浜
Sand bay.　　　　　　　　　　　　　　　　　　Sand beach.

巫山龍骨坡之龍洞
巫山竜骨坡の竜洞
Dragon cave at Longgu slope in Wushan County.

**巫山猿人遺址**　位于巫山縣西南廟宇鎮龍坪村龍骨坡。1985年至1988年,考古學家在這里發現了距今200萬年的早期人類齒骨化石。這是迄今世界發現的最早人類,有力地證明三峽地區是亞洲乃至世界人類的起源地,被命名為"巫山猿人"。

　　巫山猿人の遺跡　巫山県の西南廟宇鎮坪村竜骨坡にある。1985年から1988年まで,考古学者がここで200万年前の早期人類の歯骨化石を発現した。現在まで世界で発現された最早期の人類で,三峡地区はアジア乃至世界の人類発源地と有力的に証明,それで,"巫山猿人"と命名された。

Ruins of the Wushan ape-man. located at Longgu slope in Longping village of Miaoyu town, southwest of Wushan County. From 1985 to 1989, archaeologists have discovered fossil tooth of early man of two million years ago. It is the earliest man discovered in the world up to now. It is a strong proof that the Three Gorges region is the place of origin of man in Asia, even in the world. It was named "the Wushan ape-man."

巫山猿人遺址
巫山猿人の遺跡
Ruins of the Wushan ape-man.

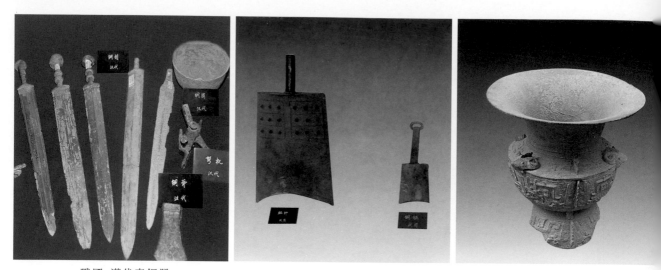

戰國、漢代青銅器
戦国・漢代の青銅器
Bronze ware of the Warring States Period and the Han Dynasty.

商代銅尊
商代の銅器——尊
Bronze wine vessel of the Shang Dynasty

**大溪文化遺址**　位于瞿塘峽東口巫山縣大溪鎮。1955年以來,考古工作者多次在此發掘出打制、磨制石器與骨器、陶器、紡輪等珍貴文物,被命名為"大溪文化"。

　　大渓文化遺跡　瞿塘峡の東口巫山県の大渓鎮にある。1955年以来,考古学者は何回もここで打制石器,磨制石器と骨器、陶器、紡織用の輪などが発掘され,"大渓文化"と命名された。

大溪鎮遠眺
大渓鎮の遠望
Distant view of Daxi town.

漢代青瓷罐
漢代の青瓷の壺
Porcelain pot of the Han Dynasty.

漢代的鎏金方銅飾
漢代の鎏金方銅器の飾りもの
Square gold-filled bronze ornament of the Han Dynasty.

明清瓷器
明清の瓷器
Chinaware of the Ming and Qing dynasties.

The ruins of the Daxi culture. Located at Daxi town of Wushan County at the east mouth of the Qutang Gorge. Since 1955, archaeologists have unearthed many times precious relics such as stoneware, bone implement, earthenware and spinning wheel etc.. It was named the Daxi Culture.

考古學家在大溪遺址進行科學發掘
考古学者は大渓遺跡で発掘している
Archaeologists conducting scientific excavation at the Daxi ruins.

大溪文化遺址
大渓文化遺跡
The ruins of the Daxi culture.

**巫山小三峡**　起于巫峡西口，沿大宁河上溯至涂家垴，全长 50 公里，由龙门峡、巴雾峡、滴翠峡三峡组成。峡区内青山回抱、碧水盈盈、流泉飞瀑，猿鸣鸟啼，玲珑而不失伟岸，妩媚中显出纯真，是一座最具自然情韵的"仙峡"，被誉为胜境中的胜境。

　　巫山小三峡　巫峡の西口から，大寧河をさかのぼって塗家垴まで全長 50 キロ，竜門峡、巴霧峡、滴翠峡の三つの峡谷からなりたっている。峡谷は青い山に抱かれ，美しく澄みきっている水が流れ，小泉が涌き，きれいな滝が青山から下へ流れ落ちて，また猿声や鳥の鳴きごえなどが聞え，玲瓏たる景色の中にその偉大さを失わず，風光明媚の中に純真が見え，もっとも自然の韻律に富む「仙峡」として勝境の中の絶景と言われている。

　　The Minor Three Gorges of Wushan. They begin at the west mouth of the Wuxia Gorge and go upstream along the Da Ning River to Tujiaba with a length of 50 km. They consist of the Longmen Gorge, the Bawu Gorge and the Di Cui Gorge. In the gorges, there are winding mountains, limpid currents, waterfalls and springs, screeching monkeys and singing birds, They are exquisite yet stalwart; charming yet innocent.

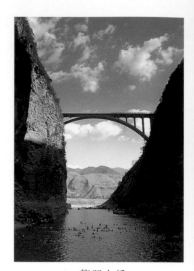

龍門大橋
竜門大橋
The Longmen bridge.

小三峡旅游船队
小三峡観光船
Touring fleet of the Minor Three Gorges.

龍門峽
竜門峽
The Longmen Gorge. 31

乳石奇觀──馬歸山
鐘乳石奇観──馬帰山
The wonder of stalacite──the Magui Mountain.

巴霧峽
巴霧峽
The Bawu Gorge.

滴翠峡
滴翠峡
The Di Cui Gorge.

寧河晚渡
寧河の晩渡り
Evening ferry at the Da Ning River.

寧河飛瀑
寧河の迫力満点の美しい滝
Flying waterfall in the Da Ning River.

撐舵
舵(梶)を取る
Punt rudder.

路漫漫
道遠く
A long, long way.

奮進
風に逆らって進む
Advance bravely.

**小小三峡** 位于大宁河支流马渡河内,是小三峡的子峡,全长 15 公里,由三撑峡、秦王峡、长滩峡组成。峡内蕨叶覆道,古藤挂空,溶洞深深,长滩幽幽,充满原始的野趣。人们游此,充分感受到回归大自然之乐。

　　小小三峡　大寧河支流の馬渡河にあり,小三峡の子峡と言われる。全長 75 キロの川には三撑峡、秦王峡、長灘峡が相次いでいる。峡谷にはわらびの葉っぱが覆っている小道,空中にかけてるすだれ深深としている溶洞、幽幽たる長い浅瀬などが見られ,原始的な趣が満ちている。人間がここまで至ると,充分に大自然に戻ったような楽しみが感じられる。

　　The Little Minor Three Gorges. (Fig.) They are in the Madu River, a branch of the Da Ning River. They are sub-gorges of the Minor Three Gorges, with a length of 15 km. They consist of the Sancheng Gorge, the Qinwang Gorge and the Changtan Gorge. There are fern-brakes covering the roads, old rattans hanging in the air, deep karst caves and secluded long beaches. All are full of primitive wild flavour. You would think that you have returned to nature and enjoy yourself to the full.

**巫山陸游洞** 位于城東3公里文峰山腰, 面向大江。洞内曲曲有徑, 大廳、回廊、弧橋、天梯……可以盡享驚與險, 奇與美的樂趣。此洞在陸游《入蜀記》中早有記載, 故名。

巫山陸遊洞 巫山県町の東約3キロ離れた文峰山の中腹, 長江に臨んでいる所にある。洞内に紆余曲折の道があり、ホール、回廊、弧形橋、険しい梯など、スリル満点に富む一方、美しさ、奇妙な感じを味わえる。この洞については、陸遊の《入蜀記》に疾っくに記載したことがあるので陸遊洞と命名したわけである。

Lu You Cave at Wushan (Fig.) located at halfway up the Wenfeng Mountain, facing the Changjiang River. There are winding paths, hall, corridor, arch bridge, climbing ladder... in the cave for you to enjoy its wonder and thrill. It was mentioned in Lu You's work "Going to Sichuan". Hence its name.

巫峽群峰
巫峽の群峰
Peaks in the Wuxia Gorge.

**巫峽**　西起重慶市巫山縣大寧河口，東至湖北省巴東縣官渡口，全長45公里。峽中峰巒競秀，雲雨變化無窮，幽深秀麗，氣象萬千，名聞遐邇的巫山十二峰即屏列其間。

　　巫峽　西は重慶市の巫山県大寧河から，東は湖北省巴東県官渡口までの約45キロの川を指す。峡谷には峰が連なり，雲雨は変化に富み，幽深秀麗で，気象万千である。天下に名を馳せている巫山十二峰がその間に並んでいる。

　　The Wuxia Gorge. It begins at the mouth of the Da Ning River at Wushan County of Chongqing City and ends at Guandukou of Badong County of Hubei province, with a length of 45km. Peaks there are beautiful with changing clouds and mists. The famous twelve peaks are all here.

巫峡秀色
巫峡のすぐれた景色
The beauty of the Wuxia Gorge.

神女峰
神女峰の夜景
The Goddess peak at night.

巫峡集仙峰
巫峡集仙峰
Jixian peak in the Wuxia Gorge.

巫峡帆影
巫峡の帆影
Reflection of sails in the Wuxia Gorge.

孔明碑　位于江北集仙峰臨江絶壁上。岩壁凹下成碑形，上鎸"重岩叠障巫峡"，訛為諸葛亮所書，故名。

孔明碑　長江北岸の集仙峰絶壁にある。岩壁が窪んで，碑の形になり，孔明筆と伝えられる「重崖畳嶂巫峡」の文字が刻まれていた。

The Kongming Tablet　located at the precipice of the Jixian Peak on the north bank of the river. A part of it caved in like the shape of tablet with inscription to the effect that the Wuxia Gorge are full of crags and peaks. It was said that Zhuge Liang wrote this tablet. But it is not true.

鏈子渓
鏈子渓
The chain creek.

楚蜀鴻溝　位于渝東最后一個小鎮——碚石鎮邊魚溪江面崖壁上，這是古人分域治里的歴史見證。而今鴻溝無溝，早已變為通途。

楚蜀の境目としての堀　重慶市東にある最後の小さい町——碚石鎮辺魚溪の江面の崖にある。これは昔の人が県と県の境目を分けて分轄する証拠である。今頃，堀がなくなり，疾っくに通い道になっていた。

The Chu shu chasm　It is on the precipice at the riverside of Baishi town, the last small town in the east of Chongqing City. This is an evidence of the ancient people's "rule by division". There is no chasm any longer today.

巫山烟雲
巫山の煙雲
Mists and clouds in the Wushan Mountains.

神女峰下青石信號臺
神女峰麓にある青石信号台
Signal post at Qingshi at the foot
of the Goddess peak.

巫峽紅橘
巫峽の赤みかん
Red tangerines in the Wuxia Gorge.

巫峡暮色
巫峡の夕日
The Wuxia Gorge in the evening.

大江東去
東へ流れていく長江
The Changjiang River runs eastward.

**巴東神農溪**　位于湖北省巴東縣長江北岸，此溪源于著名的神農架自然保護區，全長 60 公里，其中 20 公里可供漂流。它以奇特的自然風光和古樸的土家風情吸引着异域殊方的游客。

　　巴東神農渓　湖北省巴東県長江北岸にある。神農架自然保護区から発源し、全長 60 キロ。その中の 20 キロは流れにのって行くという探険ができる。奇特な自然風景と素朴の土家族風情は各地から数多くの観光客を引き寄せている。

Shen Nong creek at Badong located at the north bank of the Changjiang River of Badong County, Hubei province. It has its source in the Shen Nong Jia natural protected region, with a length of 60 km, 20 km of it can be used to drift about. It attracts the tourists with its unique scenery and simple demeanour of the Tujia minority People.

闖灘
浅瀬をさかのぼる
Rushing at the Shallows.

"碗豆角"小舟
「豌豆」形の小舟
The "pea pod" light boat.　45

屈原祠
屈原祠
Temple of Qu Yuan.

**秭歸懷古** 湖北省秭歸縣是兩位著名的才子佳人的誕生地。一位是嫻于辭令，被譽為我國詩壇之祖的愛國詩人屈原，一位是對中華民族大團結作出貢獻的"天下第一美女"王昭君。

　　秭帰で昔を思ぶ　湖北省秭帰県は才子佳人と言われる二人著名人のふるさとである。一人はわが国詩歌の先祖と呼ばれる愛国詩人の屈原。もう一人は中華民族大団結に貢献を果した「天下第一の美女」王昭君。　・

Meditation on the past at Zigui　Zigui County is the birthplave of the famous intellect and the famous beauty in Chinese history. The intellect is the eloquent patriotic poet Qu Yuan, who is praised as the father of Chinese poetry. The beauty is the "first beauty under heaven" Wang Zhao Jun who contributed very much to the unity of the Chinese nation.

屈原故里
屈原
Hometown of Qu Yuan.

香溪 香溪,是一條飄香溢美,流芳萬古的小溪,她是昭君的化身。

香溪 香溪は香りが漂う,清冽な渓流で,昭君の化身としこよく知られている。

Fragrant Creek, which leaves its mark on history and is the embodiment of Wang Zhao Jun the beauty

昭君塑像
昭君の塑像
Statue of Wang Zhao Jun.

昭君宅
昭君の宅
Residence of Wang Zhao Jun.　47

秭歸流來觀
秭帰流来観
Liulai Temple at Zigui.

西陵之秋
西陵の秋
Autumn at Xiling.

**西陵峽** 西起湖北省秭歸縣香溪口，東至宜昌市南津關，全長 66 公里，峽內險灘成陣，泡漩翻滾，江水如沸。有人謂：西陵灘如竹節稠，灘灘都是鬼見愁。岸邊石灰岩地貌發育，形成千奇百怪的景觀。

西陵峡　西は湖北省の秭帰県の香渓口から，東は宜昌市南津関まで，長さは66キロである。峡谷には険しい浅瀬が多く，渦が巻き連がり，流れは急なり，涌き水のように翻弄している。ある人の話では，西陵峡は竹の節の如く稠密で，灘灘は鬼が見ても憂う。両岸の石灰岩地貌が多く見られ，千姿万態の景観になっている。

The Xiling Gorge　It begins at the mouth of the Fragrant Creek of Zigui County of Hubei in the west and ends at Nanjiangguan of Yichang City in the east, with a length of 66 km. It is full of dangerous shallows, rolling whirpools and roaring torrents. People say: "Shallows in the Xiling Gorge are as thick as bamboo knots, and everyone of them makes the devil worry". The landform of the limestones on the river banks developed into a landscape of all kinds of strange formations.

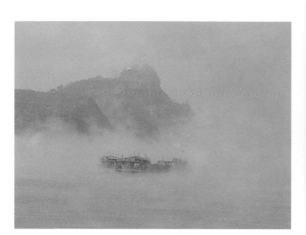

霧満峡江
霧にかすむ峡江
Fog over the river gorge.

蓮沱三把刀　位于黄陵廟下游 2 公里處,廟南一山,其山三峰相連,宛若三把利刀刺向長空。
蓮沱三本の刀　黄陵廟の下流の2キロ離れた所にある。廟南の山に三つの峰が連がり,まるで三本の鋭い刃のように空に差し向かっている。
The Three Daggers at Liantuo　It is a mountain located at the South of Huangling Temple, 2 km at the lower reaches of the temple. Its three peaks link together like three daggers pointing to the sky.

西陵夜航
西陵夜航
Night sailing in Xiling.

**宜昌三游洞**　位于湖北省宜昌市郊西陵山上。相传唐元和十四年(公元819年)白居易、元稹、白行简相约同游此洞,白居易為之作《三游洞序》。宋代、蘇洵、蘇軾、蘇轍父子三人亦同游此洞,稱"后三游"。

　　宜昌三遊洞　湖北省宜昌市郊外の西陵山にある。昔話によると,唐元和十四年(西暦819年)白居易,元積,白行簡三人がここまでに至る時,白居易が「三遊洞序」を残した。宋代に入って,蘇洵、蘇軾、蘇轍父子三人ともがまたこの洞窟に来たこともあるゆえに「後三遊」と呼ばれている。

　　San You Cave at Yichang　located in the Xiling Mountain at the west surburb of Yichang City of Hubei province. It is said that in the 14th year of Yuan He in the Tang dynasty (A. D. 819), Bai Ju Yi, Yuan Zhen and Bai Xing Jian visited this cave and Bai ju Yi wrote an account about this visit. In the Sung Dynasty, Su Xun and his two sons, Su Shi and Su Che also visited there. Fig. A corner of San You Cave.

# 三峡石韵

三峡石の韻律　　The Stone Charms in the Three Gorges

纖夫魂
纖夫の魂
Soul of the trackers.

暢游長江三峽，有雄峰萬仞直樸眼簾，有驚濤駭浪蕩滌胸臆，你自會在讀山吟水中去體味大自然的磅礴之氣，而或從山巒的啟示中去盡享男子漢頂天立地的偉力。然而，你千萬不可忽視三峽的崖岸和小小頑石，在岸邊，在江畔，那風情萬種、千姿百態的石頭會給你留下一首首凝然萬古，意韻無窮的小詩。

長江三峽下りをすると、雄大的な、険しい山峰が目に入るとともに川岸を打つ濤声も聞え、まるで胸を打つように感じている。人間はその中から大自然の宏大な気勢に対して深く感嘆する一方、大自然の奇妙さを満契できる。また山峰の啓示で男のような偉大な力を味わえるようになる。そのほか、三峡の崖岸と小さい石在忘れてはならず岸辺、江の畔、万種風情、千姿万態の石は凝然万古、韻律に富む詩歌のように散在している。

Touring in the Three Gorges, you can see the magnificient mountains and precipices, the roaring currents and frightening waves. You would enjoy the majesty of nature through its mountains and waters. But you should not neglect those little stones by the side of the precipices and the banks of the gorges. Their bearing and posture might give you an everlasting poetic charm.

石羽
石の羽
The stone plumage.

生命之源
生命の源
Origin of life.

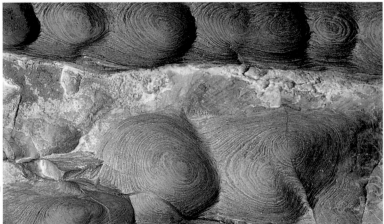

蚌群
貝の群れ
A group of clams.

鎮江石獣
鎮江の石の獣
The beast guard of the river.

石靈芝
石のさるのこしかけ
The stone magic
fungus.

滴水穿石
雨だれ石を穿つ
Little drops penetrate
the rocks.

大自然的雕塑
大自然の塑像
Sculpture of nature.

石浪
石の浪
The stone wave.

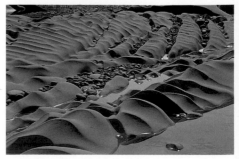

年輪
年紋
The annual ring.

冰川
氷河
The glacier.　59

萬卷書
万冊の書
Volumes of books.

石林
石林
Stone forest.

傲骨
骨
The unbending backbone.

岁月
岁月
Years of time.

61

# 三峽百萬大移民

三峽百万人の立ち退き　　*The Migration of a Million People in the Three Gorges*

　　三峽工程的成敗，首要問題是移民。據測算，正常蓄水175米，將淹沒重慶市、湖北省所轄19個縣市，淹沒人口72.55萬，最終動遷人口將達113.38萬，不亞于一個小國的搬遷，這是一道世界級的大難題。當前，我國在移民工作中，已探索出開發性移民的路子，一期水位移民已按時順利完成。未來十年將進行更大規模的移民。歷史，將以敬重、同情的目光，關注那些"為大家、舍小家"的庫區兒女。

　　三峽ダム建設の成敗は立ち退きの問題である。測算により，正常蓄水水位は175mに達すると，重慶市、湖北省管轄下の19の県、市，72.55万の人々が水沉される。最終移住する人口は113.38万に達する。これは小さい国の全体引っ越しにあたっている。確かに世界級の大難題である。現在，国は立ち退きの仕事を進める中にはもう開発型移住というやり方ができた。一期水位線に住んでいる人人はもう時間通りに移住した。未来の10年間，大規模な移住作業が進んで行くと見ている。歴史は尊敬，同情の見方で「国家のために家を捨てる」ダム地区の人々に注目を集める。

The success of the Three Gorges Project first depends on the migration　It is estimated that the water storage capacity level set at 175 meters will inundate 19 cities and counties of Chongqing City and Hubei province with a population of 725, 500. The population to be finally migrated will be 1, 133, 000, no less than the migration of a small country. This is a difficult problem of the world level. The state hsa now explored a way to conduct the migration work. Migration at the first stage of inundation has been sucessfully completed. Migration on larger scale will be carried on in the coming ten years. History will show respect to people in the Reservoir region.

搬遷前的湖北省秭歸縣周坪鄉巨坊村
引っ越し前の湖北省秭帰県周坪郷巨坊村
Jufang village in Zhouping country-town of Zigui
County of Hubei province before migration.

搬遷后的巨坊村
引っ越し後の巨坊村
Jufang village after migration.

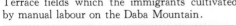

移民們用勤勞的雙手在大巴山上開墾的梯田
移住者は勤勉な両手で開拓していた大巴山
の段々畑
Terrace fields which the immigrants cultivated
by manual labour on the Daba Mountain.

移民們搬進新居
引っ越し中の移住者
The immigrants move into their new homes.

63

三峽庫區淹没城市和部分淹没城市。
三峡ダム地区水没される町と一部分水没される町
Cities inundated or partly inundated in the Reservoir Region in the Three Gorges:

| | |
|---|---|
| 1 長壽縣<br>長寿県<br>Chang Shou County. | |
| 2 涪陵<br>涪陵<br>Fuling city. | 5 萬縣<br>万県市<br>Wanxian city. |
| 3 豐都縣<br>豊都<br>Fengdu County. | 6 開縣<br>開県<br>Kaixian. |
| 4 忠縣<br>忠県<br>Zhongxian. | 7 雲陽縣<br>雲陽県<br>Yunyang County. |

8 奉節縣
奉節県
Fengjie County.

9 巫山縣
巫山県
Wushan County.

10 巫溪縣
巫溪県
Wuxi County.

11 巴東縣
巴東県
Badong County.

12 秭歸縣
秭帰県
Zigui county.

13 興山縣
興山県
Xingshan County.

14 宜昌縣太平溪
宜昌県太平溪
Taipingxi of Yichang.

# 大壩雄姿

西陵長江大橋遠眺
西陵長江大橋の遠望
Distant view of the Changjiang bridge at Xiling.

1919 年，一代偉人孫中山提出在三峽"以閘堰其水""資其水力"的宏偉構想；

1956 年，歷史巨人毛澤東發出"更立西江石壁，截斷巫山雲雨，高峽出平湖"的千古絕唱。

爾后，考察、論爭長達三十多年。1981 年 1 月 4 日，作為未來長江三峽水利樞紐的重要組成部分，葛洲壩水利樞紐工程攔江大壩勝利截流。1992 年 4 月 3 日，第七屆全國人大第五次會議通過關于興建三峽工程的決議。1997 年 11 月 8 日大江截流成功。于是，世界第一大壩即將聳立在華夏大地，成為三峽地區最壯麗的景觀。

1919 年，偉人である孫中山が三峡で「閘門を作って水をためる」、「水力を利用する」というすばらしい構想を提出した。

1956 年，歷史の巨人である毛沢東は「更に西江石壁を立ってっ巫山の雲雨を断り，平湖は高峡から出る」という千古の絶唱も提出した。

その後，視察，争論が 30 年あまり続いた。1981 年 1 月 4 日未来の長江三峡ダムの重要部分としての葛洲壩ダムの長江せきとめが完成した。1992 年 4 月 3 日，全国第七回全国人民代表大会の第五次会議では三峡ダムを建設する決議を通過した。1997 年 11 月 8 日三峡ダム長江をせきとめする工事が成功した。将来，世界一のダムは中国の大地で聳え立ち，三峡地区の景観がもっとも壮麗な所と見られている。

In 1919, Dr. Sun Yat-sen put forward a magnificient concept of "barring the water with a dam" and "making use of the water resources".

In 1956, Chairman Mao Tse-tung wrote the everlasting poem of "establishing a stone wall in the west over the Changjiang River to cut off the clouds and mists in the Wushan Mountains and let a smooth lake appear among the high gorges".

Since then, investigations and controversies continued for more than thirty years. On January 4, 1981, as an important component of the water control project of the Three Gorges of the Changjiang River, the Gezhouba Water Control Project successfully dammed the Changjiang River. On April 3, 1992, the fifth Plenary Session of the Seventh People's Congress passed the resolution to construct the Three Gorges Project. On December 11, 1997, the Changjiang River was successfully dammed. Thus, the first huge dam in the world will stand firmly in China and become the most majestic view in Sanxia (the Three Gorges) district.

**葛洲壩水利樞紐** 位于湖北省宜昌市西郊長江干流上,大壩全長 2561 米,建有兩座水電站,總容量 217.5 萬千瓦,年發電約 141 億度。建有船閘 3 座,可通過萬噸級大型船隊。

**葛洲壩ダム** 湖北省宜昌市の西郊長江の本流にある。ダムは全長 2561メートル。二つの水力発電所が建てられ、設備総容量は217.5万 kW。年発電量は約 141 億 kWである。ロックゲートは三つあり,万トン級の大型船が通過できる。

**The Gezhouba Water Control Project** It is located on the mainstream of the Changjiang River at the west surburb of Yichang City of Hubei province. The dam is 2,561 meters long. There are two hydropower stations with total capacity of 2.125 million kilowatts. Its annual electric energy production is about 141,000 million kilowatt/hours. Three sluice gates were built there to let ships of ten thousand tonnage pass through.

雄偉的葛洲壩水利樞紐
雄大な葛洲壩ダム
The magnificient Gezhouba Water Control Project.

船閘一景
ロックゲートの姿
A scene in the sluice gate.

**舉世無雙的三峽工程** 正在興建的長江三峽工程是當今世界上最大的水利工程。建成后，總體容量達 393 億立方米，其中防洪庫容 221.5 億立方米，裝機容量 1768 萬千瓦，年發電 840 億度。這是惠及當代，澤被子孫的宏偉大業。

**世界唯一の三峽ダムプロジエクト** 現在,建設している長江三峽ダムは今現在世界で最大な水利プロジエクトである。完成後,総容量は393億立方メートルになり,洪水防御の容量は221.5億立方メートル,設備総容量は1768万KWで,年発電量は840億KWである,これは恵みは当代に,子子孫孫までも受益の宏大な工事である。

**The un-rivalled Three Gorges Project** The Three Gorges Project under construction is the largest water control project in the world today. When completed, its total capacity will be 393,000 million cubic meters. Installed capacity will be 17.68 million kilowatts. Annual electric energy production will be 840,000 million kilowatt. It is a magnificient enterprise beneficial to the present generation as well as to posterity.

大江截流前一天之中堡島(此片攝于 1997 年 11 月 7 日)
長江をせきとめる前日の中堡島(1997 年 11 月 7 日撮影)
Zhong Bao Dao on the day before the river was dammed (Photo taken on December 7, 1997).

三峡大坝坝址——中堡岛原貌
三峡ダムの工事現場——水没前
の中堡島
Site of the dam —— Zhong Bao
Dao before inundation

繁忙的施工運輸碼頭
忙しい工事現場の運送埠頭
Wharf where the transport is busy.

大壩施工工地一隅
工事現場の一角
A corner of the construction site.

# 三峡風情

三峡風情　Feelings of the Three Gorges

老船
老船
The old boat.

　巫山猿人與大溪文化透出三峡文明的曙光，歷史用鋒利堅韌的刻刀在這片土地上鐫出獨具風韵的三峡文化，釀就獨具三峡特色的民俗風情。那甜甜的峡聲、峡語，無不展示出巴山女兒的健美與嫵媚；那悠悠的山歌、船號，無不顯露三峡漢子的粗獷與豪爽。是滔滔大江蕩滌出他們的靈性，是巍巍高峡磨煉了他們的品格。崖岸的篙點與石上的足痕展示出他們生生不息、頑強抗爭的偉力。而今，溫馨的陽光已穿過高峡深谷，照進他們世世代代堆砌的吊腳樓，于是他們打開沉重的家門，撲向五彩繽紛的世界。

　巫山猿人と大渓文化は三峡文明の曙が見え、歴史は鋭い刃のようでこの土地に独特な三峡文化を刻み上げ、そして、三峡あたりの特色がある民俗風情を育てた。甘美な三峡の声、三峡の言語はいずれも巴山女児の美しさと婀娜を展示し、あの素朴な山歌、船頭たちの喚声は三峡男性の力強さと豪快さを展示している。とうとうたる長江はかれらの霊知を作り、巍峨な高い峡谷はかれらの人柄を育成した。崖岸にあるふな竿の跡、石に残した足跡はかれらがいきいきし、一生懸命に争う力を表わす。今，温かい日さしが高峡谷を通して、かれらが世世代代築いてきた吊脚楼に差し込んでいる。これから、重いドアを開けて、多彩な世界へ向う。

　　The Wushan ape-man and the Daxi culture dawned on the civilization of the Three Gorges. History has worked out its culture and its unique folk custom. The sweet voices and talks demonstrate the vigour and grace of the Bashan girls. The carefree folk songs and boatman's songs exhibit the toughness and proud of the Three Gorges fellows. Today, the warm sunshine has penetrated into the high gorges and deep valleys and shined on their traditional houses. They come out of their clumsy doors and plunge into the multi-coloured world.

織
織み
Weaving.

巴山女
巴山女
The Bashan girl.

巴山漢子
巴山若い男性
The Bashan man.

碼頭搬運工
埠頭のポーター
The dockers.

騾隊
騾馬
A file of mules.

受冷落的"時裝模特兒"
目もくれない「ファッションモデル」
The coldly treated "Fashion model".

相親相愛
愛しあう
Getting on well together.

73

遠山的呼唤
遠山の呼声
The calling of the distant mountains.

人間
人間
The human world

農家
農家
The peasant's home.

牧羊曲
牧羊曲
The shepherd's song.

牛郎
牛を放牧する男性
The cowboy

江邊的故事
江道の物語
Riverside story.

峡江漁翁
峡江の魚つりおじいさん
The fisherman in the gorge.

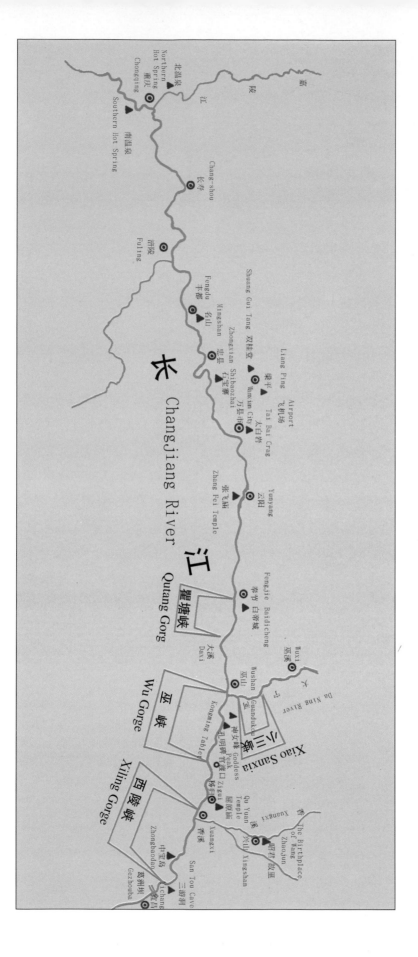

三峡旅游示意图
TOURIST MAP OF THE THREE GORGES